JUNETEENTH
MIDDLE SCHOOL

SOCIAL STUDIES WORKBOOK

THE ACHIEVERS BOOK SERIES

ISBN: 979-8-9901854-1-8

UNTRADITIONAL PUBLISHING COMPANY, LLC

ST. LOUIS, MO

ORDERS@THEACHIEVERSBOOKS.COM

THEACHIEVERSBOOKS.COM

The Achievers Book Series

Untraditional Publishing Co, Est. 2011

Grades Pre-K to 1

Foundational Skills

GRADES PRE-K TO 1

FOUNDATIONAL SKILLS WORKBOOK

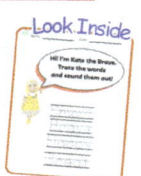

Look Inside

Grades 1 t

Reading Literature

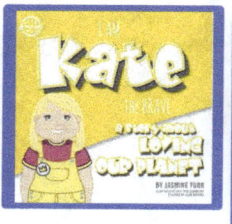

THE ACHIEVER ELA WORKBO

Look Inside

For the wor
get all five
or mix and

Grades 3 to 5

Reading Literature

Look Inside

Look Inside

ROADTRIP BROS ELA WORKBOOK
GRADES 3-5

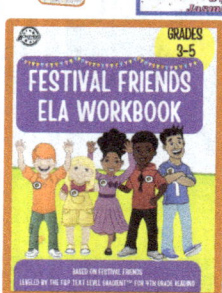

FESTIVAL FRIENDS ELA WORKBOOK
GRADES 3-5

Grades 6 to

Social Studies

Look Inside

JUNETEENTH MIDDLE SCHOOL SOCIAL STUDIES WORKBOOK

JUNETE HIGH SCH SOCIAL STUDIES

JUNETEENTH ELEMENTARY SCHOOL SOCIAL STUDIES WORKBOOK

- Four disciplines
- C3 Framework
- For social studies requir
  only the workbook is ne

EMAIL
PURCHASE ORDER
Orders@TheAchieversBooks.com

 OR

BUY NOW
TheAchieversBooks.com

TABLE OF CONTENTS

Lesson	Topic	Discipline	C3 Theme
1	What is Juneteenth & Freedom	History, Civics	time, continuity, and change; power, authority, and government
2	Maps	Geography	people, places, and environment
3	1 Order, 2 Acts 3 Amendments	Civics	power, authority, and government
4	Juneteenth and Opal Lee	History	time, continuity, and change
5	How We Can Celebrate	Economics	production, distribution, and consumption

Directions: read the text and answer the question.

Name _____   Date _____

WHAT IS JUNETEENTH

**Juneteenth celebrates
the freedom of humans, primarily of African
descent.** The holiday marks the end of
generational, chattel slavery where people were
held against their will

Freedom is the ability to
act, speak, or think as one wants without restraints

America is known as The Land of the Free. **What are
some things you are free to do after school?**
(example: play soccer, visit family or friends). List below:

_____

_____

_____

_____

_____

Name _____   Date _____

JUNETEENTH & INDEPENDENCE

Juneteenth (June 19, 1865) celebrates the freedom of people who used to be enslaved. The Declaration of Independence (July 4, 1776) marks the separation from Great Britain. Both holidays celebrate our freedoms.

Circle the quotes from the Declaration of Independence that support the celebration of Juneteenth:

ALL MEN ARE CREATED EQUAL

[THE RIGHT TO BE] FREE AND
INDEPENDENT STATES

[PEOPLE HAVE A RIGHT] TO LIFE, LIBERTY
AND THE PURSUIT OF HAPPINESS

[AGREEING TO JUST] LAWS IS
WHOLESOME AND NECESSARY FOR THE PUBLIC GOOD

Name _____ Date _____

UNION AND CONFEDERATE STATES DURING THE CIVIL WAR

The Civil War, where the Union fought against the Confederacy, was from 1861 to 1865. The primary focus of the war was the economic and moral issues around slavery. The result was freedom for the millions of humans who were enslaved.

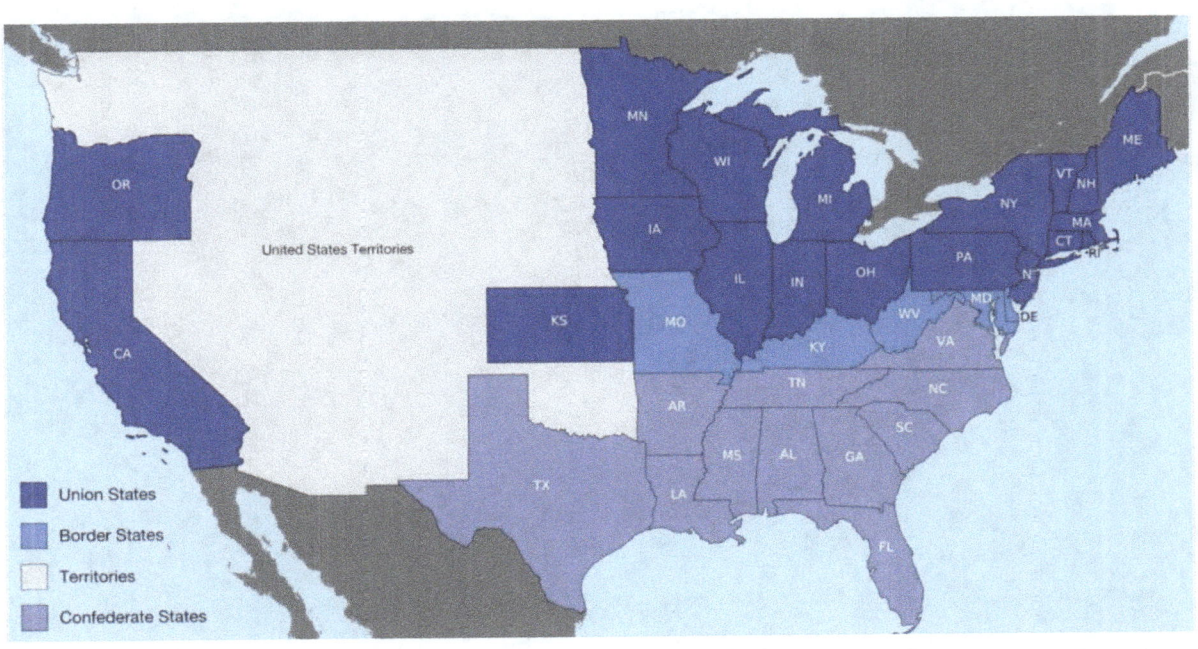

Where were the Union states primarily located?

_____

_____

Name _____   Date _____

TEXAS STATE MAP

The Emancipation Proclamation
stated that all the enslaved humans were free. It was
issued on January 1, 1863. Then, **the General Order
Number 3 was issued in Galveston, Texas, on June
19, 1865,** freeing the last 250,000 humans who were
still wrongfully enslaved in Texas. **This day is
remembered as Juneteenth.**

Galveston

**How would you travel to send a message to
Galveston, TX?**

_____

_____

Directions: read the text and write.

Name _____ Date _____

QUOTE FROM GENERAL ORDER NUMBER 3

> The people of Texas are informed that, in accordance with a proclamation from the Executive of the United States, all slaves are free. This involves an absolute equality of personal rights and rights of property between former masters and slaves...*

 **Let's pretend that you are a general. Write an order declaring the freedom of your class to go to a park with your families after school:**

_____

_____

_____

_____

_____

*"Juneteenth". Texas State Library and Archives Commission.

Name _____   Date _____

AMENDMENTS & ACTS

In 1865,
the **13th Amendment**
abolished slavery

In 1868,
the **14th Amendment** gave citizenship
to all people born in the US

In 1870,
the **15th Amendment** gave Black
Americans the right to vote

The **Civil Rights Act of 1964** prohibited
discrimination based on race, color,
religion, sex or national origin

The **Voting Rights Act of 1965** outlawed
discriminatory voting practices

If given the chance, **what school rule would you amend?**
(example: students can bring pets)

_____

_____

Directions: read the text and answer the questions.

Name _____ Date _____

TIMELINE

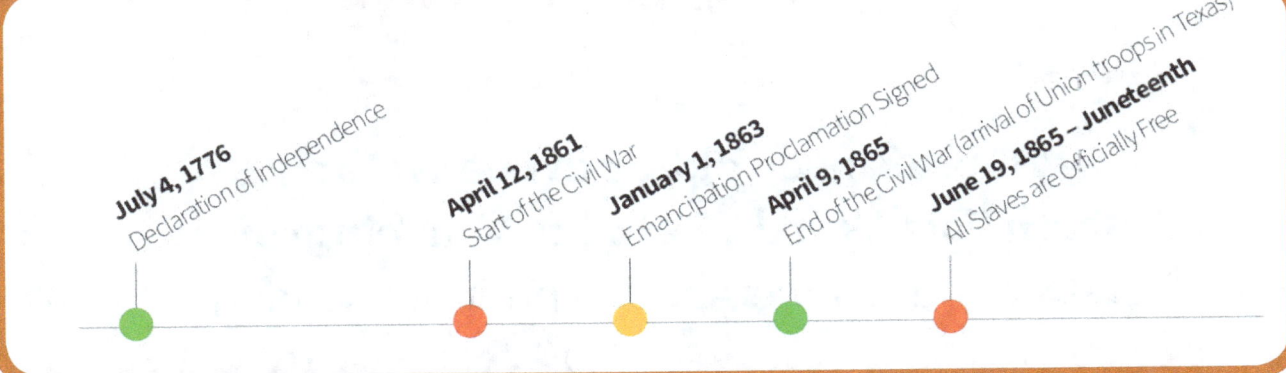

July 4, 1776
Declaration of Independence

April 12, 1861
Start of the Civil War

January 1, 1863
Emancipation Proclamation Signed

April 9, 1865
End of the Civil War (arrival of Union troops in Texas)

June 19, 1865 – Juneteenth
All Slaves are Officially Free

During the time between the Emancipation Proclamation and Juneteenth, there were people enslaved that should have been free. How do you think each group of people felt during this time, and why?

The people who were free:

The people enslaved:

Abolitionists (people who wanted to stop slavery):

The people who owned enslaved people:

Directions: read the text and answer the question.

Name _____ Date _____

OPAL LEE AND BECOMING A NATIONAL HOLIDAY

In 2016, 89-year-old **Opal Lee walked from Fort Worth, Texas to Washington, DC** to make Juneteenth a national holiday.

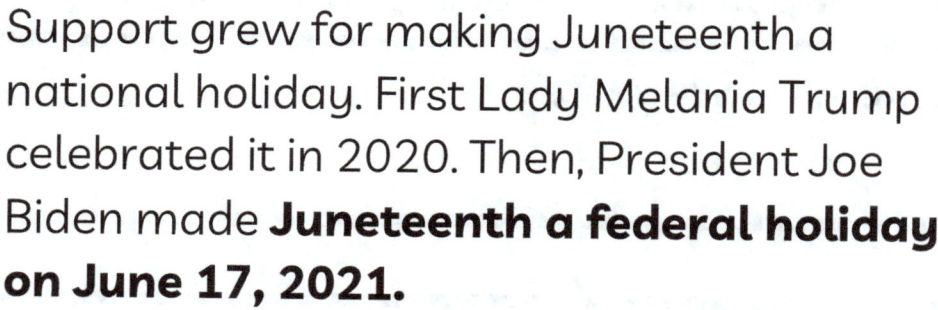

Support grew for making Juneteenth a national holiday. First Lady Melania Trump celebrated it in 2020. Then, President Joe Biden made **Juneteenth a federal holiday on June 17, 2021.**

If given the chance, **what day would you make a federal holiday?** (example: your birthday)

_____

_____

_____

Photo by: David Perry

Name _____ Date _____

JUNETEENTH CELEBRATIONS

The first Juneteenth in 1866 was celebrated with food, singing, and church-centered gatherings. There are so many ways to celebrate Juneteenth today: Party at the park or backyard, festival, live music or dance performance, BBQ, cookout, cook traditional foods, parade, pageant, talent show, outdoor games, make a display of relevant books at a local library, support a local business, reading, movie.

Let's pretend that you are hosting a Juneteenth celebration. Create an invitation:

You're Invited!
Juneteenth Celebration
Day: June 19
Time:
Place:
What to Expect:

Name _____ Date _____

HOW WE CAN CELEBRATE JUNETEENTH

Juneteenth brings more opportunities for local black-owned businesses that participate in the holiday. This includes businesses such as event spaces, restaurants, clothing companies, authors, etc. This celebrates the transition from generational slavery to generational freedom and wealth.

1. If you **start a business, what products or services would you offer**?

_____

_____

2. Is there a **local black-owned business in your city?** If so, what are their products or services? (examples: bookstore, I'm not sure)

_____

_____

Name _____   Date _____

TEST YOUR KNOWLEDGE

1. When was the original Juneteenth?	a. June 19, 1865 b. June 19, 1965 c. June 9, 1865 d. June 9, 1965
2. Where was the original Juneteenth?	a. St. Louis, MO b. Jacksonville, FL c. Galveston, Texas d. New York, New York
3. In 2016, this person walked from Fort Worth, Texas to Washington, DC to make Juneteenth a national holiday. What is the name of this person?	a. Oprah Winfrey b. Opal Lee c. Rosa Parks d. Martin Luther King Jr.
4. When did Juneteenth become a federal holiday?	a. June 17, 1865 b. January 1, 1970 c. January 1, 1999 d. June 17, 2021

answer key: 1. (a) 2.(c) 3.(b) 4.(d)

Name _____ Date _____

TEST YOUR KNOWLEDGE

13th Amendment

gave Black Americans the rig
to vote

14th Amendment

gave citizenship to all people
born in the US

15th Amendment

abolished slavery

Directions: draw a line to match each holiday to its definition.

Name _____ Date _____

TEST YOUR KNOWLEDGE

Juneteenth

celebrates the passage of the Declaration of Independence and the separation from Great Britain

Independence Day (4th of July)

celebrates a prominent leader in the civil rights movement and encourages the reflection of racial equity

Martin Luther King Day

celebrates the freedom and liberty of human beings, primarily of African descent and the abolishment of slavery

www.ingramcontent.com/pod-product-compliance
Lightning Source LLC
Chambersburg PA
CBHW080859120626
46553CB00009B/2685